13 Colonies

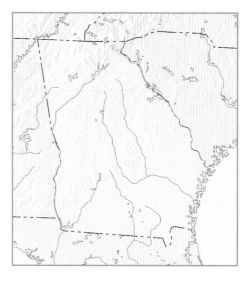

GEORGIA

13 Colonies

GEORGIA

THE HISTORY OF GEORGIA COLONY, 1732–1776

ROBERTA WIENER AND JAMES R. ARNOLD

Chicago, Illinois

© 2005 Raintree
Published by Raintree,
A division of Reed Elsevier, Inc.
Chicago, IL

For information, address the publisher:
Raintree, 100 N. LaSalle, Suite 1200, Chicago, IL 60602

Printed and bound in China

08
10 9 8 7 6 5 4 3 2

Library of Congress Cataloging-in-Publication Data
Wiener, Roberta, 1952-
  Georgia / Roberta Wiener and James R. Arnold.
       p. cm. -- (13 colonies)
Includes bibliographical references (p.) and index.
Contents: Georgia in 1733 -- A unique vision -- Beginnings in Savannah
-- The colony expands -- The Spanish war -- Everyday life -- Revolution
-- Glossary.
  ISBN 0-7398-6879-9 (lib. bdg.) -- ISBN 1-4109-0303-6 (pbk.)
  ISBN 978-0-7398-6879-9 (lib. bdg.) -- ISBN 978-1-4109-0303-7 (pbk.)
  1. Georgia--History--Colonial period, ca. 1600-1775--Juvenile
literature. 2. Georgia--History--Revolution, 1775-1783--Juvenile
literature. [1. Georgia--History--Colonial period, ca. 1600-1775. 2.
Georgia--History--Revolution, 1775-1783.] I. Arnold, James R. II.
Title. III. Series: Wiener, Roberta, 1952-   13 colonies.
  F289.W55 2004
  975.8'02--dc22
                              2003021148
                              2003011056

Title page picture: The best plantations in Georgia were located along the tidewater and freshwater swamps that ran inland for about 20 miles (32 kilometers) along rivers and streams.

Opposite: Farmers made clearings in woodlands, and planted the cleared land with crops.

The authors wish to thank Walter Kossmann, whose knowledge, patience, and ability to ask all the right questions have made this a better series.

Some words are shown in bold, **like this.** You can find out what they mean by looking in the glossary.

Picture Acknowledgments

Architect of the Capitol: 6-7 Authors: 20 Mark Catesby, *The Natural History of Carolina, Florida, and the Bahama Islands*, 1771: 15 Colonial Williamsburg Foundation: Cover, 18, 23, 45 bottom, 47 bottom, 50, 56 top Georgia Historical Society, Savannah, Georgia: 29, 39, 54, 55 Gibbes Museum of Art/Carolina Art Association: Title page, 48, 52-53 Courtesy of Hargrett Rare Book & Manuscript Library/University of Georgia Libraries: 11, 19, 25, 41, 46, 47 top, 51 Historical Society of Pennsylvania: 10 Eric Inglefield: 14, 43, 59 Library of Congress: 5, 9, 16, 17 top, 21, 22, 24, 26-27, 28, 30 bottom, 31, 32-33, 36-37, 38, 44, 45 top, 49, 56-57, 58 Benson J. Lossing, *Our Country: A Household History of the United States*, 1895: 17 bottom National Archives: 8, 13 National Park Service, Colonial National Historical Park: 34-35 I. N. Phelps Stokes Collection, New York Public Library: 30 top

Contents

PROLOGUE: THE WORLD IN 1732

By the year 1732, the year British colonists sailed for Georgia, twelve British colonies already existed in what would become the United States of America. Europeans had been exploring the wider world for more than 200 years. Advances in navigation and the building of better sailing ships had made longer voyages possible. Great sailors from Portugal, Spain, Italy, the Netherlands, France, and England had sailed into uncharted waters. The explorers reached Africa, India, the Pacific Ocean, China, Japan, and Australia. There they encountered kingdoms and civilizations that had existed for centuries.

Europeans saw great opportunity in these distant lands. They saw the chance to grow rich from trade in exotic spices. They saw souls ready to be converted to Christianity. They saw the chance to make conquests and expand their countries into great empires. And not least, they encountered the dark-skinned people of Africa and, thinking them a different species, saw the chance to capture and sell slaves.

All the voyagers from Europe to the lands of the Pacific Ocean had to sail around Africa, a long and dangerous journey. So European explorers began to sail westward in search of a shorter way. In 1492, the explorer Christopher Columbus landed on an island on the far side of the Atlantic Ocean and claimed it for Spain. He thought that he had actually sailed all the way around the world and come to an island near India. Years of exploration by numerous sailors passed before the people of Europe realized that Columbus was the first European of their era to set foot in a land unknown to them. They called this land the New World, although it was not new to the people who lived there. In 1507 a mapmaker gave the New World a new name—**America**. Though they did not give up looking for a shortcut to Asia, explorers from Spain, France, and England sailed to North and South America and began to claim large pieces of these lands for their own nations.

Spanish explorers and conquerors went on to destroy two Native American empires in America—the Aztecs and the Incas. They brought the first domestic horses to the Americas, and established a printing press and a university. They explored much of South and Central America and the southern part of North America.

AMERICA: LAND THAT CONTAINS THE CONTINENTS OF NORTH AMERICA AND SOUTH AMERICA

The first Europeans to walk on the soil of what is now Georgia came in 1540. In that year the Spanish explorer Hernando de Soto led a military expedition into Georgia while searching for gold. His soldiers clashed with Cherokee and Creek Native Americans. Many Native Americans died from European diseases that they caught from the Spanish.

De Soto's expedition created interest in North America's southeastern region. Both Spain and France

An unrealistic image shows Spanish explorer Hernando de Soto reaching the Mississippi River. He did so only after fighting his way through resistance from Native Americans in Alabama and Mississippi.

MISSION: PLACE IN A
FOREIGN LAND
ESTABLISHED BY PEOPLE
TRYING TO SPREAD THEIR
RELIGION, USUALLY
CHRISTIANITY

claimed the territory that is now Georgia. In 1565 the Spanish settled St. Augustine, Florida, the first permanent city in the future United States.

The following spring, a Spanish conquistador, Pedro Menéndez de Aviles, traveled north to explore the coast. Menéndez encountered a Native American chief named Guale on an island off the Georgia coast. The Spanish named the island Guale (modern-day St. Catherines) and left thirty soldiers to build a fort. This fort was the first permanent European settlement in Georgia.

The Spanish practice was to send missionaries to convert the Native Americans to Roman Catholicism. In 1566 Jesuit friars founded **missions** on St. Catherines and the Cumberland Islands. Franciscan missionaries followed and expanded the area of Spanish influence. The Guale people did the manual work to feed and support the Spanish.

In 1597 a Guale chief told his people that the missionaries were preparing the way for Spanish colonists to take the Native Americans' land and force them into slavery. The Native Americans revolted. Spanish authorities in nearby Florida responded with military force and squashed the rebellion. In 1606, a Spanish bishop confirmed more than 1,000 Guale as true Catholics.

For the next fifty years Spanish influence spread along the Georgia coast and inland along the Chattahoochee River. When the English king Charles II granted territory

De Soto landed in Florida, bringing with him Spanish horses, and traveled overland to explore parts of Georgia.

St. Augustine was the first permanent European settlement within the boundaries of the present day United States. It also became the major base for Spanish Florida. In 1587, the English admiral Sir Francis Drake burned St. Augustine. Drake's attack caused the Spanish to withdraw from Georgia to concentrate on defending their remaining possessions in Florida.

in the Carolinas to the English lords in 1663, the scene was set for conflict between England and Spain. Georgia was one of the battlegrounds. In the 1680s the Yuchi, Creek, and Cherokee joined with the English to attack the Spanish missions in Georgia. These attacks drove the Spanish back to Florida. Georgia became a disputed land between the Spanish settlements in Florida and the English settlements in South Carolina.

A series of wars involving the Spanish and English and their Native American allies began in 1702. Over the next

A Cherokee chief

several years, an army of South Carolinian colonists and their Native American allies ventured south through Georgia to raid communities of Native Americans who were loyal to the Spanish. The army burned Native American villages and captured thousands of Native Americans to be sold into slavery, destroying about three quarters of the Native American population in Spanish territory. South Carolina leaders began to plan for English settlements in Georgia to protect South Carolina from both the Native Americans and the Spanish. The South Carolinians were particularly interested in preserving their profitable trade with the Native Americans who lived to the west and south. The spread of French settlements along the Gulf Coast also threatened the Native American trade. The French threat provided another reason for the British to settle Georgia.

The South Carolina **assembly** made a detailed military report in 1720. The assembly recommended settlements in Georgia at the falls of the Savannah River and at the mouth of the Altamaha River. Both places were good for Native American trade and were surrounded by excellent farm land. Colonel John Barnwell of South Carolina built Fort King George at the mouth of the Altamaha River in 1721. The fort burned down four years later and was not rebuilt. So Georgia remained without any permanent European settlements until 1733. By that time, British settlements stretched from present-day Maine to the Savannah River, and these settlements were home to more than half a million European colonists and about 90,000 slaves.

I.
GEORGIA IN 1733

Georgia has three geographic regions: Appalachian Highlands; Piedmont; and Coastal Plain. The highlands are a mountainous region that includes the southern end of the Blue Ridge and Appalachian Mountains, as well as Georgia's highest point, the 4,784-feet (1,458-meter) high Brasstown Bald Mountain. Limestone valleys and ridges are found in the northwestern part of the state.

ASSEMBLY: LOWER HOUSE OF A LEGISLATURE, WITH DELEGATES ELECTED BY THE VOTERS

The place where the rivers form waterfalls as they descend from the hills is known as the Fall Line. In Georgia the Fall Line marks the southern boundary of the Piedmont region.

The land generally slopes downhill from the northern highlands to the Atlantic coast in the southeast. Between the mountains and the coast is a hilly region called the Piedmont. Rolling hills cover a high flatland, or plateau, made of rock. Veins of red or gray clay color the soil in this area, so land is typically called "red land" or "gray land."

The flat Coastal Plain makes up the southern half of Georgia. There the soil is a mix of sand, sandy loam, and some clay. There are many swamps and marshes along the rivers leading to the sea. The best known wetland is the Okefenokee Swamp along the border with Florida. Georgia's Atlantic Ocean coastline stretches about 100

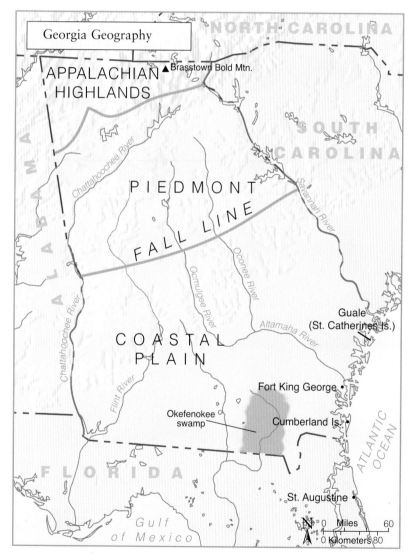

Georgia is the largest state east of the Mississippi River.

Georgia's best known wetland is the Okefenokee Swamp along the border with Florida.

miles (161 kilometers). Offshore are islands that shield the coast from Atlantic storms.

About half of Georgia's streams flow to the Atlantic, including its two main rivers, the Savannah and the Altamaha. Most of the other half, including the Chattahoochee and Flint, are in western Georgia and flow south to the Gulf of Mexico. The Savannah River forms Georgia's border with South Carolina.

Because of its location near both the Gulf of Mexico and the Atlantic Ocean, Georgia has many rainy days. The average yearly rainfall is 50 inches (127 centimeters). The oceans also influence the temperature and humidity. The Coastal Plain and Piedmont are warm and humid with hot summers and mild winters. The mountainous north has lower temperatures and humidity. Tropical storms and hurricanes often approach the Georgia coast.

Because Georgia's land runs from the mountains to the sea it has an unusually diverse range of natural vegetation. When

Europeans came to Georgia they found it heavily forested. Soil types and elevation influence plant and animal diversity. Cypress trees live along the coast. Oak and pine grow along most of the coastal plain, giving the area its colonial name of "the pine barrens." As the land rises, sugar maple and beech grow. Oak and poplar dominate the Appalachians.

The Atlantic wetlands provide a nursery for fish and shellfish. Many reptiles and amphibians, including alligators, live in marshs and swamps. Deer, bears, foxes, and opossums roam the woods.

NATIVE PEOPLES

Native Americans lived in Georgia more than 10,000 years before the arrival of the first Europeans. When Europeans first came to Georgia, the major Native American tribe living along the coast was the Guale. The Guale belonged to the Muskogean linguistic family. By the time the British arrived, Spanish pressure and attacks from Native Americans living to the north had driven the Guale away from the Georgia coast.

Georgia's major tribes at the time of European contact were the Yuchi, Creeks, and Cherokees. The Yuchi lived along the Savannah River and formed a unique linguistic stock. They were apparently a warlike people who terrorized most of the tribes living along the coast. However, Shawnee attacks drove them from the Savannah River. Small bands later returned to their homeland, and the British governor guaranteed them their rights to their own land until their resettlement in 1751.

The Creeks originally lived along the Georgia coast. Conflicts with Europeans

English naturalist Mark Catesby painted pictures of North American wildlife in the 1720s. Ibises are wading birds that live in coastal wetlands. An English visitor wrote that ibises "are as white as milk, and fly very slowly".

Opposite: Semitropical forest in coastal Georgia

caused them to move inland. The name Creek became attached to a loose organization of tribes known as the Creek Confederacy. The Creeks lived in towns extending from the Georgia coast inland all the way to central Alabama. The Creeks were the most powerful group living close to the first British settlements. Because the Creeks held a central position between British, Spanish, and French colonies, each of these European powers tried to win the favor of the Creeks. After a war with the Yamassees in 1715, the Creeks moved to the Chattahoochee River. Here they remained until the early 1800s.

The Cherokees lived in mountainous northern Georgia. They were friendly with the British and were important trading partners. This powerful tribe shielded Georgia settlers from attack by Native Americans living to the north.

Among the Cherokee and Creek peoples, women, children, and old men farmed. Corn was the main crop. The younger men were hunters and warriors. Deer, buffalo, and turkey provided meat.

Most European artists had an unclear notion about how southeastern Native Americans lived. This drawing supposedly shows a group of Florida Native Americans hunting crocodiles. Actually, few crocodiles live in Florida, but alligators were common both there and in Georgia.

2.
A UNIQUE VISION

James Oglethorpe was born in 1696. His father was an army colonel. Oglethorpe attended Oxford University and then served with a European army where he gained military experience. He returned home to live on the family estate outside of London. Oglethorpe was elected to Britain's **Parliament** in 1722, but a more important experience came six years later.

In England, a person who could not pay his bills could be thrown into **debtors'** prison. Once there, a prisoner had to bribe corrupt wardens to treat him better than other prisoners, or else suffer under miserable conditions. A good friend of Oglethorpe's was confined to debtors' prison and could not afford to pay the warden, so he was kept with prisoners who had smallpox, and died of the disease. As a result, Oglethorpe used his position in Parliament to begin an investigation of the jails in Great Britain.

Oglethorpe's efforts led to the arrest of some of the worst prison wardens. His investigation also exposed the dreadful prison conditions and caused Parliament to free about 10,000 inmates, mainly debtors. To celebrate Oglethorpe's efforts, a clergyman published a poem that included the lines:

Yet Britain cease they Captives' Woes to mourn,
To break their Chains, see Oglethorpe was born!

James Oglethorpe left Georgia in 1743 and never returned. He lived until 1785. Shortly before his death, he expressed feelings of friendship and respect for the new United States.

PARLIAMENT: LEGISLATURE OF GREAT BRITAIN; IT HAS AN UPPER HOUSE, THE HOUSE OF LORDS, AND A LOWER HOUSE, THE HOUSE OF COMMONS

DEBTOR: PERSON WHO OWES A DEBT, USUALLY MONEY

British prisons of the 1700s were dark, damp, cold breeding grounds for deadly illnesses.

UTOPIA: IMAGINARY PLACE WITH A PERFECT SOCIETY AND GOVERNMENT

TRUSTEES: GROUP OF PEOPLE ENTRUSTED WITH THE MANAGEMENT OF AN ORGANIZATION OR A PIECE OF PROPERTY

GREAT BRITAIN: NATION FORMED BY ENGLAND, WALES, SCOTLAND, AND NORTHERN IRELAND; "GREAT BRITAIN" CAME INTO USE WHEN ENGLAND AND SCOTLAND FORMALLY UNIFIED IN 1707.

King George II and his Privy Council had to approve all Georgia laws.

Oglethorpe became famous in religious and charitable circles, where he met like-minded men. They worried about what was to become of the people released from debtor's prison. They decided to sponsor a charity colony in America. This vision led to the founding of Georgia, named after Britain's King George II.

Of all the thirteen colonies, Georgia was unique. The founders wanted a **utopian** society, by which they meant a society where people lived as perfectly as possible. The founders formed a group and called themselves **Trustees**. The Trustees would provide leadership. But unlike leaders in other colonies, none of them could make money from the colony or even own land there. Instead, they saw the work of creating a utopian society in Georgia as an act of charity.

The Trustees' main goal was to make Georgia a place where very poor British people could settle and prosper. In **Great Britain**, the poor were a burden on society. They were often beggars and thieves. The Trustees thought that they could send poor people to Georgia where they could earn a living.

Once the colony became established, the Trustees thought Georgia could help Great Britain's economy. In particular, the Trustees thought that Georgia could produce silk and wine. In the 1730s, Great Britain bought silk and wine from other countries. These purchases were expensive. If instead Georgia provided silk and wine, the money would benefit Britain. Another reason the Trustees wanted to create a colony in Georgia was for military purposes to protect South Carolina's people and trade.

The original 21 Trustees who founded Georgia included ten members of the British House of Commons, two members of the House of Lords, and five Church of England ministers. The Trustees possessed valuable experience that helped Georgia become established. Some, like Oglethorpe, had long been active in charitable work. Others were wealthy enough to provide money for the colony or knew wealthy people who could give financial help. The Trustees who were members of the House of Commons were especially important because the Commons provided most of the money to support the colony.

In 1732 the Trustees received formal approval for the Georgia charter. The charter established Georgia's original

Georgia Silk

When the Trustees proposed a colony in Georgia, they argued that silk manufacture would support the colony. Each year Britain paid 500,000 British pounds to import silk. If this trade could be transfered to Georgia, both England and the colony would benefit enormously. The Trustees knew that the first colonists were city dwellers with no knowledge of agriculture. But they thought that raising silkworms was an easy job.

Silk is a fiber produced by certain caterpillars who use it as a building material for cocoons. Mulberry trees provide the leaves that silkworms eat. The *Ann*, a British ship, carried silkworm eggs among its cargo. Mulberry trees came to Savannah the next year. Each colonist had to plant 500 mulberry trees for each fifty acres of land they received. Women received special rewards when they learned to unwind the silk thread from the cocoons.

What seemed like an easy business to the Trustees in London proved difficult in reality. Late frosts often killed the leaves needed for food for the silkworms. People failed to care for the mulberry trees. Many eggs failed to survive the voyage from Europe. The special equipment needed to manufacture silk was in short supply.

With all these problems, Georgians still managed to manufacture some high-quality silk.

Supposedly, Georgia silk was used to make a dress for the queen of England in 1735. The best silk year during the Trusteeship was 1751 when Georgia exported just under 500 pounds. This total was far too little to be of great value.

Silkworm cultivation. The shelves hold mulberry leaves to feed the worms.

MILITIA: GROUP OF CITIZENS, NOT NORMALLY PART OF THE ARMY, WHO JOIN TOGETHER TO DEFEND THEIR LAND IN AN EMERGENCY

INDENTURED SERVANT: PERSON WHO HAS AGREED TO WORK AS A SERVANT FOR A CERTAIN NUMBER OF YEARS IN EXCHANGE FOR FOOD, CLOTHING, A PLACE TO SLEEP, AND PAYMENT OF ONE'S PASSAGE ACROSS THE ATLANTIC TO THE COLONIES

boundaries as between the Savannah and Altamaha Rivers and westward to the Pacific Ocean. It made the Trustees responsible for everything except command of the **militia**. The governor of South Carolina was to control the militia. In case the Trustees abused their position, the charter had several safeguards. It was to last for only 21 years.

The Trustees made a detailed plan for the colony that also made it unique. They did not sell land, but gave it to the deserving poor. No one would be allowed to own large amounts of land. Everyone except **indentured servants** would own between 50 and 500 acres. In other words, the colony's population would be made up of small farmers. All the settlers would have to work. Slavery was forbidden because the Trustees believed that owning slaves would lead to larger plantations like those in South Carolina. Small farmers would be unable to compete with large plantations worked by slaves.

The Trustees carefully selected the first settlers. These settlers were the deserving poor, people who through no fault of their own had fallen on hard times and were willing to work. They supported most of the first group by providing everything they thought the settlers would need, such as tools and seeds. In the language of the time, this support was called "on the charity." In addition, some of the first settlers paid their own expenses so that they could join the expedition to Georgia. Whether the settlers paid their own way or were on the charity, the reason they went to Georgia was to obtain free land.

On November 16, 1732, a group of Trustees traveled to the English port of Gravesend. They boarded the sailing ship *Ann* for an inspection. They reported that the ship was in good order to carry the settlers to Georgia. The next day the *Ann* set sail. A total of 114 passengers were on board.

A modern replica of a sailing ship's main mast . The trustees who inspected the *Ann* reported that it was "Tight & Strong & well Manned, Tackled," meaning its sails and ropes were in good condition. They concluded that the *Ann* was suitable to carry the first Georgia settlers across the Atlantic.

3.
BEGINNINGS IN SAVANNAH

The voyage across the Atlantic went smoothly. On February 12, 1733, the colonists arrived at Yamacraw Bluff, 17 miles up the Savannah River. The Yamacraws were a small band of about 100 outlawed Creek Native Americans. Oglethorpe reported that the Yamacraws were "a little Indian Nation, the only one within Fifty Miles," and that they were friendly and "desirous to be Subjects to his Majesty King George." The Yamacraw chief, Tomo-Chi-Chi, welcomed the settlers with great ceremony. Tomo-Chi-Chi and Oglethorpe made speeches and exchanged gifts. Unlike the first settlers in the other colonies, the Georgia settlers had little fear of Native American attack.

On Yamacraw Bluff, Oglethorpe directed the construction of a settlement called Savannah. It included a fort and wooden walls for defense that enclosed the town. Outside of the walls, settlers cleared land to plant crops.

The town plan featured an orderly pattern of straight streets and regular public squares. To this day the public squares remain a notable feature of Savannah life. House lots measured 60 by 90 feet (18 by 27 meters), and fronted on a street and backed on an alley. Each block had ten lots. Four blocks, called tithings, made up a ward. Each ward had a public square at its center. All the houses were built the same. Skilled black laborers brought from South Carolina cut pine trees and shaped the timber. The pine-framed houses measured 24 by 16 feet (7 by 5 meters) and had roofs of tarred

Oglethorpe meets with the Yamacraws.

Tomo-Chi-Chi, chief of the Yamacraws, is shown here with his son. Tomo-Chi-Chi remained a friend to the colonists for the rest of his life. He died in 1739 at the age of 100 and received the honor of a British military funeral. He was buried in Savannah at his own request.

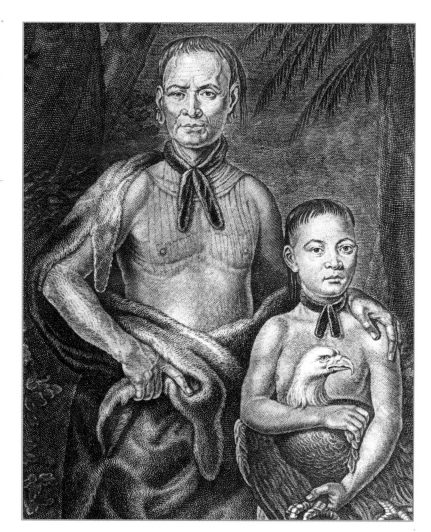

The man who drew this plan for the building of Savannah, Peter Gordon, came to Georgia on the *Ann*. He had worked as an upholsterer in England. Gordon returned to England in 1734 and presented the drawing to the Trustees, who "seemed pleased with it, and ... ordered me a small present."

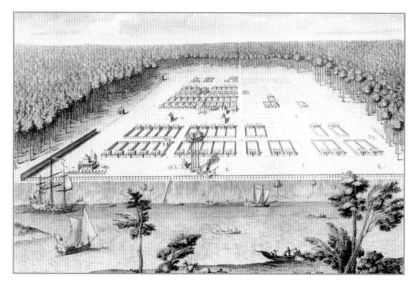

shingles. The inside was one simple room with a sleeping loft overhead.

Construction went well. A visitor from South Carolina reported that Oglethorpe worked tirelessly and was "extremely well beloved by all his People." The settlers usually called him "Father." Proof of Oglethorpe's dedication to others' welfare is the fact that he was one of the last people to move from a tent into a house. He had made sure that everyone was taken care of before he thought of himself.

The colonists were all city dwellers. Only three of them knew anything about growing crops. Fortunately, South Carolina provided gifts of food and the Yamacraws gave the new colonists meat. Even though the construction of Savannah went well, the colonists still faced diseases that they did not understand. The first to die was the colony's only physician.

In July, at least 60 settlers were sick at the same time. The colony was in near panic. A stroke of good luck occurred when a ship arrived unexpectedly. It carried 42 Jewish settlers who had come from

Above: Of the 114 colonists who left England aboard the *Ann*, 29 died within a year and 47 within ten years. The *Ann* had also carried the colony's doctor and a chest of medicines.

Left: Colonial medicine bottles. Colonial doctors did not understand the diseases that sickened and killed Georgia's settlers. Oglethorpe blamed the deaths on the colonists' fondness for rum.

INQUISITION: STATE-SPONSORED PERSECUTION OF NON-CATHOLICS IN SPAIN AND PORTUGAL, NOTED FOR THE USE OF TORTURE

England, including Doctor Samuel Nunis. Nunis went to work immediately to help the sick. All of Nunis's patients recovered, although a total of 20 colonists died the first summer, possibly of diseases carried by mosquitos or contaminated water.

The colony's organizers did not want to let the Jewish settlers stay. Nunis's work greatly helped persuade the British to tolerate the Jews, and Oglethorpe admitted them anyway. By the time Savannah was one year old it had a population of 437. Close to one in ten inhabitants was Jewish. They were a mix of German Jews and Sephardic Jews from Portugal and Spain. The Sephardic Jewish people especially wanted to see Georgia grow to challenge the Spanish, whom they hated because of Spain's persecution of Jews during the **Inquisition**.

THE COMPLAINTS BEGIN

Settlers built simple cabins on their farms, and few could afford the luxury of windows.

The Trustees thought of themselves as kindly fathers who, out of the goodness of their hearts, were helping the poor. In many ways they treated the settlers like children. The Trustees expected the settlers to be thankful for what the Trustees were doing. Instead, the settlers complained.

It began the first summer. Oglethorpe traveled to Charles Town, South Carolina, and when he returned he found the people changed. Oglethorpe blamed the change on alcohol. He wrote that they had started to drink heavily and become "disobedient so that at my return I hardly knew them." It got worse. The settlers wanted more of everything and were unhappy with all the restrictions. They did not want to work hard or to follow the rules. Oglethorpe reported that he "could not revive the Spirit of Labour: Idleness and Drunkenness was Succeeded by Sickness." What Oglethorpe did not realize was that the colonists were enjoying the freedom they found in Georgia. They were unwilling to follow his orders blindly. They no longer considered Oglethorpe their "Father."

The Trustees believed that alcohol had created an enormous problem among the London poor. In London, people could buy a gallon of gin for one penny. Cheap gin produced a large population of men and women who lived only to drink alcohol. They could neither perform useful work nor care for their children. Instead, they often became beggars and robbers in order to buy alcohol. So the Trustees tried to prevent the colony from importing alcohol, particularly rum.

The Trustees claimed that they did this to keep the Creek Native Americans from causing "great disorders" because of drunkenness. In fact, they wanted to prevent the white colonists from drinking too much. But a British trader who lived near Savannah had ample rum stocks and there was nothing Oglethorpe could do about it. The conflict between the Trustees and the colonists was a sign of things to come.

Some people ridiculed Oglethorpe's idealistic plan for settling Georgia. This cartoon portrayed a settler being flown to Georgia on an airship powered by geese.

4.
THE COLONY EXPANDS

Savannah grew slowly, and Oglethorpe planted new settlements in adjacent areas. Most settlers found life outside of Savannah too lonely and isolated. Several of the new settlements failed. However, the Trustees also opened Georgia to settlement by select, non-British groups. Georgia offered religious freedom to all except Roman Catholics. Some groups seeking religious freedom successfully built new settlements.

The first came from the Salzburg area in central Europe. The **Archbishop** of Salzburg tried to convert his

ARCHBISHOP: A HIGH-RANKING MINISTER WHO HAS AUTHORITY OVER A CHURCH DISTRICT

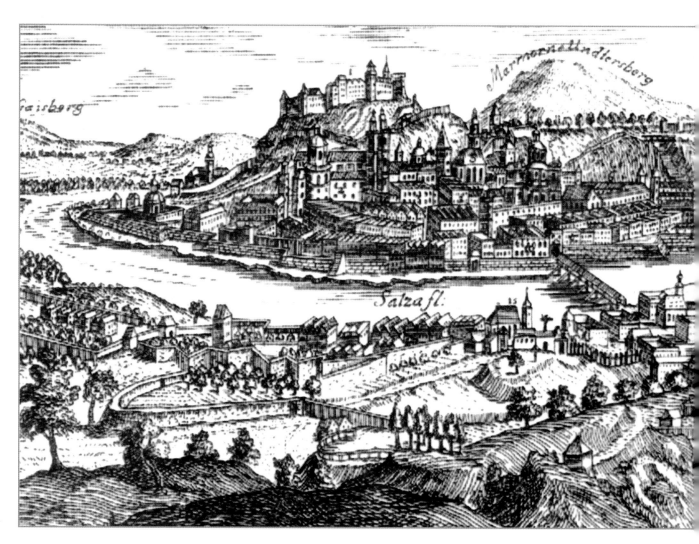

Lutheran subjects to Roman Catholicism. Some 30,000 Lutherans chose to leave instead of converting. Great Britain was the leading **Protestant** state in Europe and so took an interest in helping the Salzburger refugees. Parliament granted the Trustees a large sum to assist the Salzburgers. In October 1733, 78 Salzburgers began the long journey to Georgia.

Oglethorpe guided the Salzburgers to a location 22 miles (35 kilometers) north of Savannah. The Salzburgers named their settlement Ebenezer, the Rock of Help in the Bible. The location proved to be a poor choice. Numerous Salzburgers fell sick. The land was not very productive and it was very hard to move freight back and forth to Savannah. After two years of struggle, the Salzburgers insisted that they be

> LUTHERAN: BELONGING TO THE PROTESTANT CHURCH BASED ON THE IDEAS OF MARTIN LUTHER, A 16TH-CENTURY GERMAN MONK WHO QUESTIONED CATHOLICISM
>
> PROTESTANT: MEMBER OF ANY CHRISTIAN CHURCH THAT HAS BROKEN FROM AWAY FROM ROMAN CATHOLIC OR EASTERN ORTHODOX CONTROL

Salzburg, Austria, as it appeared in a 1732 illustration for a book about the Lutheran emigration.

Salzburgische Emigranten.

*Nichts, als das Evangelium
Vertreibt uns ins Exilium.
Verlassen wir das Vaterland,
So sind wir doch in Gottes Hand.*

A 1732 book illustration of Salzburg emigrants leaving Austria for Georgia. The verse says that having left their home country, they are in God's hands.

MORAVIAN: MEMBER OF A CHRISTIAN CHURCH FIRST FORMED IN MORAVIA, IN EASTERN EUROPE, DURING THE 1400S

allowed to move their town to a better location six miles (10 kilometers) away. Here they slowly prospered. Ebenezer grew from 130 people in 1738 to about 250 by 1742.

The success of the Salzburgers encouraged the Trustees. They offered land to another German-speaking group of religious refugees, the **Moravians**. The first Moravians came to Georgia in 1735, but most moved to Pennsylvania within a few years because other Georgians did not share their antiwar beliefs. However, additional German-speaking peoples continued to come to Georgia. By the 1770s there were close to 3,000 Germans who lived in tightly knit communities where they shared language and religion.

Opposite: The Salzburgers arrived off the Georgia coast on a Sunday that was a special Lutheran holy day. One Salzburger wrote, "All was cheerful on board. It was really edifying to us that we came to the borders of the promised land, this day, when as we are taught … from the Gospel, that Jesus came to the borders of the seacoast, after he had endured persecution and rejection by his countrymen."

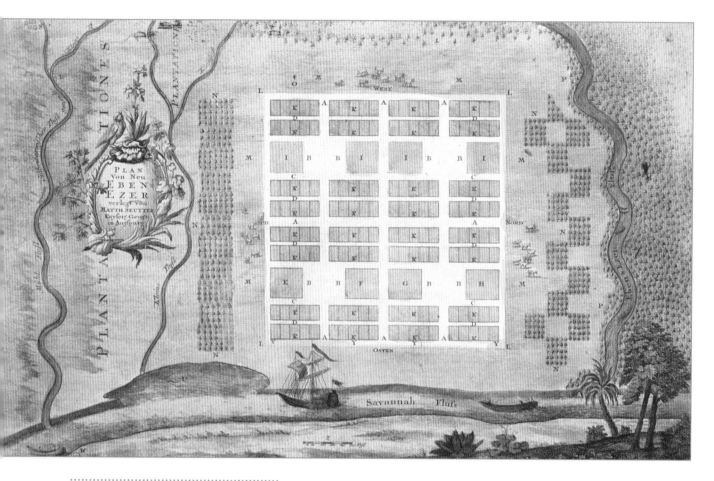

Above: A plan for the Salzburger settlement, Ebenezer

Right: The Moravians were **pacifists**. When war with Spain drew near, they left Georgia and sailed north to Pennsylvania.

To show his liking for Georgia's Scottish Highlanders, Oglethorpe sometimes wore Highland dress when he visited them.

Between 1732 and 1741, the Trustees also paid the way for 1,810 people to come to Georgia. This group included mostly British people including Scottish Highlanders but also 800 foreign Protestants, mostly German, Swiss, or Austrian. During the same period another 1,021 people paid their own way to Georgia, and most of them were also British.

During the time the Trustees controlled Georgia, most people lived in towns and villages rather than in the countryside. Charity settlers received 50 acres, divided into a lot for a home in town, a five-acre garden plot just outside of town, and about 45 acres farther away to be used for farming. Each charity colonist received food, clothing, tools, and seeds to get started.

After clearing the fields, the farmer had to prepare the soil. Stumps and roots made plowing difficult, so most of

the preparation involved backbreaking work with a hoe. Then the seeds had to be planted. An experienced colonist warned that until the farmer became used to the hot climate, he would spend more money on doctors than he could earn from his farm.

There was a great deal that the colonists did not know about how to live in Georgia. Too few people knew how to build a sound structure. For example, within about ten years, termites had destroyed all of the original homes built in

Savannah. A potter built Savannah's first wharf in 1739. It was not well built and soon collapsed. As late as 1754, when the colony's first royal governor, John Reynolds, met with his **council**, the chimney at one end of the council house collapsed.

The Trustees created a fund for "Encouraging and Improving Agriculture" in the colony. Friends of the colony contributed a variety of plants, including mulberry trees, olive trees, grapevines, cotton, hop roots, coffee berries, tea plants, orange trees, hemp, and flax. A gardener planted them in a ten-acre plot outside of Savannah known at the Trustees' Garden. Some plants thrived while others sickened and died.

COUNCIL: GROUP OF ADVISORS, SIMILAR TO THE UPPER HOUSE OF A LEGISLATURE, APPOINTED BY A COLONIAL GOVERNOR

A South Carolina planter explained to a Trustee what was necessary to start a farm in Georgia: "The Planter ... must first build himself a house or hut, next he goes to clearing, which is done by hewing the underwood, and then falling the trees and lopping off their Branches. When he thinks he has cut down as much as he can clean and enclose before Planting time, he cross cuts some of the Trees, and Splits them into rails for his fences, and then destroys the rubbish that lies upon his fields."

The mulberry trees, essential for silk manufacture, were one of the successes. But quarrels among the garden's caretakers, a bad frost in 1738, and an unusually hot summer combined to ruin the garden. By 1741 only a few fruit trees remained.

The Trustees' Garden was one of many examples of a noble idea gone wrong. The Trustees had thought that silk and wine manufacture would be particularly profitable for Georgia. Neither activity worked as planned. Silk manufacture proved too difficult. European grapevines

The Trustees suggested that 20,000 workers could be employed making silk in Georgia. Events proved them wildly optimistic.

did not thrive in Georgia's soil and climate, so the colony never made very much wine.

The Trustees also expected Georgia to grow enough food to feed all the colonists. But among the early settlers, only the Salzburgers understood agriculture. The Trustees' store in Savannah had to supply food during the first years and again whenever poor growing years occurred. The Trustees had expected that poor British townspeople would not be happy doing the hard work necessary for

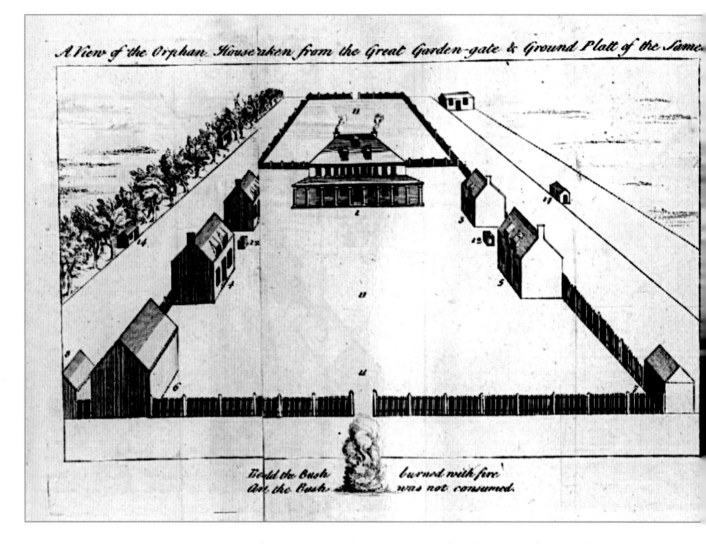

A View of the Orphan House taken from the Great Garden-gate & Ground Platt of the Same

farming. So, they promised the charity colonists that farm work in Georgia would be easier than in Britain because "the climate is so much kinder and the soil so much more fruitful." This was obviously an exaggeration.

In 1738 the colony's population of settlers was between 2,000 and 3,000. Yet only about 1,000 acres had been cleared, which was not enough to feed everyone. Also, the ignorant settlers often tried to plant crops that were simply wrong for the soil and climate. Much of the soil was sandy and infertile. Europeans had never experienced anything like Georgia's long, hot summers. Corn provided the main food crop. Peas, potatoes, and garden vegetables were also grown easily. The Salzburgers grew and harvested rice, but until slaves came to Georgia, rice production was low.

AN
ACCOUNT
OF
Money Received and Disbursed
FOR THE
ORPHAN-HOUSE
IN
GEORGIA.

By GEORGE WHITEFIELD, A.B.
Late of Pembroke-College, Oxford,

To which is prefixed
A PLAN of the BUILDING.

LONDON:
Printed by W. STRAHAN for T. COOPER at the *Globe* in *Pater-noster-row,* and Sold by R. HETT at the *Bible* and *Crown* in the *Poultry.* 1741.
[Price Sixpence.]

1. Orphan-House.
2. Infirmary.
3. Work House.
4. Kitchin.
5. Wash House.
6. Cart House.
7. Intended to be a Still House.
8. Stable.
9. Intended for a Store House.
10. Necessary Houses.
11. Court Yard.
12. Wells.
13. Great Garden, gate.
14. Workmens Huts in the Woods.

Scale of English feet.

N: Jones del.

Because most charity colonists proved unable or unwilling to do farm labor, the colony made great use of indentured servants. The indentured servants included English, Irish, Scottish, and Germans. The Georgia settlers bought the indentured servants and worked them until their contracts, or indentures, were completed. By 1741 indentured servants made up about 20 percent of the population. During the years 1733 and 1752, private individuals held 2,492 indentured servants.

The Trustees supported a combination orphanage and school for poor children in Savannah. In 1740 the institution was moved 10 miles (16 kilometers) to Bethesda.

NATIVE AMERICAN RELATIONS

In 1734 Oglethorpe invited Tomo-Chi-Chi and his wife along with some other Native Americans to accompany

Charles Wesley, an Anglican minister, spent a few months in Georgia in 1736 preaching to Native Americans.

him on a voyage to England. Oglethorpe wanted to use the Native Americans to create attention for Georgia. At the same time he wanted to impress Tomo-Chi-Chi with British power. Tomo-Chi-Chi met the king, the Trustees, and the Archbishop of Canterbury. The meetings were a great success.

Oglethorpe and Tomo-Chi-Chi returned to Georgia, where the Native American leader continued to help the British colonists. When he died in 1739, Oglethorpe ordered a formal British military ceremony. Tomo-Chi-Chi was buried in Savannah. He had been a respected and valuable friend to the British.

During the colony's early years, Georgia produced little of trading value. Before the colony was settled, South Carolina traders had developed a profitable trade with the Native Americans. The traders exchanged manufactured items for animal skins, especially deerskins. Once Georgia became established, the South Carolina Native American traders were eager to establish trading bases in Georgia. However, Oglethorpe and the Trustees denied the South Carolinians land because they objected to using rum to trade with the Native Americans.

Yet the Trustees also needed to keep peace with the Native Americans. So, in 1735 the colony began to issue trading licenses. Trade with the Native Americans led to the founding of Fort Augusta at the falls of the Savannah River. Augusta quickly became a center for Native American trade and the colony's second most important town.

In 1739 Oglethorpe traveled about 300 miles (483 kilometers) into the wilderness to negotiate a lasting peace treaty with the powerful Creek Nation. The Creeks agreed to remain loyal allies to the British and ceded a large amount of land for white settlement. For Oglethorpe and for Georgia, this treaty was a major diplomatic triumph.

During all of Oglethorpe's Native American negotiations, he received help from a remarkable woman named Mary Musgrove. She was part Native American and the wife of a trader who had established a post near

Savannah. She served Oglethorpe by acting as an advisor and translator.

Georgia had few worries about Native American attacks. This was largely because Oglethorpe established excellent relations with the Yamacraw leader Tomo-Chi-Chi. Tomo-Chi-Chi and Mary Musgrove acted as a diplomatic link between the British and the powerful tribes such as the Creeks who lived to the west. When she was released, she traveled to London and appealed to the British authorities. She eventually settled for a small sum of money and ownership of St. Catherines Island.

Mary Musgrove's third husband was Thomas Bosomworth, an Anglican minister. Bosomworth gave up the ministry and moved to his wife's trading post. The couple caused a great deal of trouble by claiming rights to vast lands. At one point Mary declared herself Queen of the Creeks. In 1749 the Bosomworths came to Savannah with a menacing group of Creeks to demand payment for her past services to Oglethorpe. The incident ended with her arrest.

5.
THE SPANISH WAR

Georgia's growth slowed dramatically as the threat of war with Spain increased. In October 1739 Great Britain formally declared war on Spain. The news was announced in Savannah in May 1740. Oglethorpe had proved a fine leader during times of peace. The war with Spain tested his military skills.

The Spanish War went by the name of the "War of Jenkins' Ear". The Spanish coast guard had caught an English smuggler named Thomas Jenkins. The Spanish treated Jenkins roughly and he lost his ear. This treatment outraged many British. But Jenkins' ear was merely an excuse for the war. Great Britain and Spain really went to war because they each wanted to control the slave trade with the **West Indies**. In addition, Great Britain and Spain argued about the Georgia-Florida boundary.

Oglethorpe had expected a war with Spain. Back in 1737 he had asked Parliament for money and men to defend Georgia. Parliament granted 20,000 British pounds and Oglethorpe personally recruited a 700-man regiment while he was in England. Parliament also named Oglethorpe military commander for both South Carolina and Georgia.

Oglethorpe returned to America, where he strengthened Georgia's defenses and worked to make alliances with the Native Americans. Conflict in Georgia came in mid-November 1739 when the Spanish raided the coast. Oglethorpe responded with raids into Spanish Florida.

Next, Oglethorpe prepared for a major attack against St. Augustine. He gathered 500 of the soldiers he had recruited in Britain, companies of Scottish and English rangers, 600 South Carolinians, and about 1,100 Native Americans. This was a sizeable and impressive force for the time. He also made arrangements to cooperate with British warships.

On May 9, 1740, Oglethorpe began his **campaign**. The Spanish stoutly resisted Oglethorpe's invasion. Oglethorpe began a **siege** of St. Augustine in hopes of starving out the **garrison**. Just when it seemed the city would surrender, three small Spanish ships slipped past the British ships to deliver food. Oglethorpe could not maintain the siege.

WEST INDIES: ISLANDS OF THE CARIBBEAN SEA, SO CALLED BECAUSE THE FIRST EUROPEAN VISITORS THOUGHT THEY WERE NEAR INDIA

CAMPAIGN: SERIES OF ACTIONS TAKEN TO REACH A MILITARY GOAL

SIEGE: CAMPAIGN TO CAPTURE A PLACE BY SURROUNDING IT, CUTTING IT OFF FROM SUPPLIES, AND ATTACKING IT

GARRISON: SOLDIERS STATIONED AT A FORT TO PROTECT IT

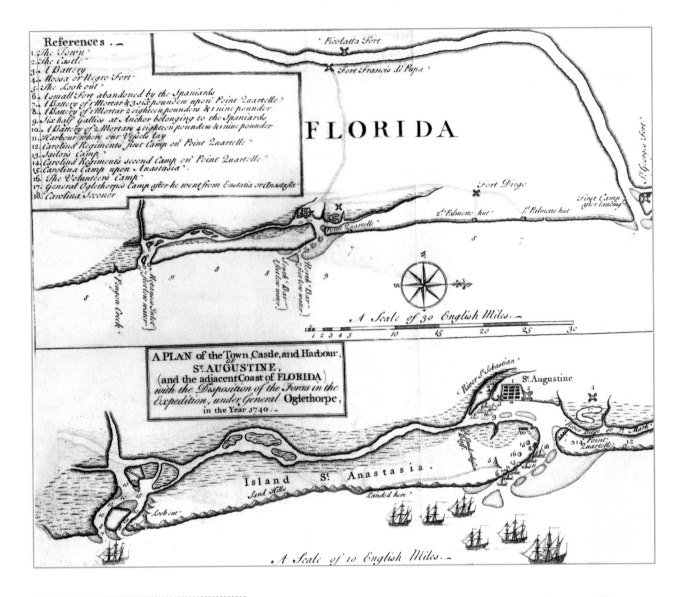

A map showing Oglethorpe's attack on St. Augustine.

Sickness, the threat of hurricanes, and unwillingness among the South Carolinians and Native Americans to continue, forced him to retreat on July 20.

Little happened in Georgia until the summer of 1742, when the Spanish invaded. They marched against the town of Frederica, where the Battle of Bloody Marsh took place on July 7. Oglethorpe won a hard-fought battle and the Spanish eventually withdrew. Oglethorpe declared a day of thanksgiving "for this great deliverance, and the end that it put to this Spanish invasion." He received much praise for his victory. Seven colonial governors sent him letters of congratulation.

Class Structure

Slaves were at the bottom of Georgia's class structure. Slaves served as both laborers and artisans. In addition to working the fields and acting as servants, they made all the common things necessary for a plantation. They manufactured and laid bricks, cut trees and shaped them into useful lumber, and made simple tools in the forge. Masters had the power of life and death over their slaves, and masters who killed their slaves often went unpunished. A slave could not expect to improve his place in society. Very few masters freed their slaves. Historians estimate that there were never more than 20 to 40 adult free blacks in Georgia at any time before 1775. Everyone else in Georgia had a chance to rise or to fall in social class. Social position mostly depended on wealth. In all of the free classes, men had more privileges and more legal duties than women.

After slaves, indentured servants were the lowest class. Like slaves, their contracts were bought and sold, and like slaves, many performed the hardest labor in the colony. However, they received better food and clothing than the slaves. Unlike slaves, though, when their work contract was completed, usually in seven years, they became free. Still, the rest of society looked down on indentured servants "the very scum and refuse of mankind." After slaves came to Georgia, people looked down on indentured servants even more, because slaves could replace servants as workers.

Georgia had a small class of free white laborers. They stood above indentured servants, even though they performed the same kind of work, simply because they were free. But they could hardly compete with slave labor, since slaves did the same work as laborers. Free white laborers did not make up a large part of society.

The overseers who managed plantations were above the common laborers. Most overseers received salaries and often shared in a plantation's profits. An overseer named William May signed a typical contract in 1769 that paid him 25 pounds for the year and allowed him "a third part of the Hogs he Raises on the plantation and also half of the Poultry." By colony law, there was supposed to be a white overseer present on

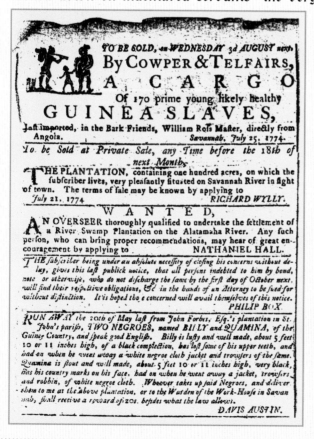

An advertisement for a slave sale in Savannah.

any plantation that had slaves. Some people ignored this law and used a trustworthy slave as overseer.

Next highest in class were the skilled craftsmen, called mechanics in colonial times. To be successful the mechanics had to do better work than slaves. Mechanics worked at many occupations including blacksmithing, carpentry, shoemaking, and leather tanning.

Professional men such as schoolteachers, clergymen, medical men, and lawyers were above the skilled craftsmen. Merchants fit in above the skilled craftsmen too, but whether they were social equals to the professional men depended upon their wealth.

Unlike in Europe, there were no nobles in Georgia. So, at the top were the so-called "gentlemen." A person became a gentleman by possessing a fortune, holding an important office, or by being highly respected through word and action. As best as they could, Georgia gentlemen tried to act like men of the landowning class in Britain. They showed off their wealth and enjoyed a high standard of living. As a sign of their status, like British gentlemen, they had the privileges of hunting and fishing on all open lands, and of performing their military service on horseback.

Above right: In the language of the time, a blacksmith was considered a skilled mechanic.

Right: Gentlemen of Georgia enjoyed hunting on all open lands in the style of English gentlemen.

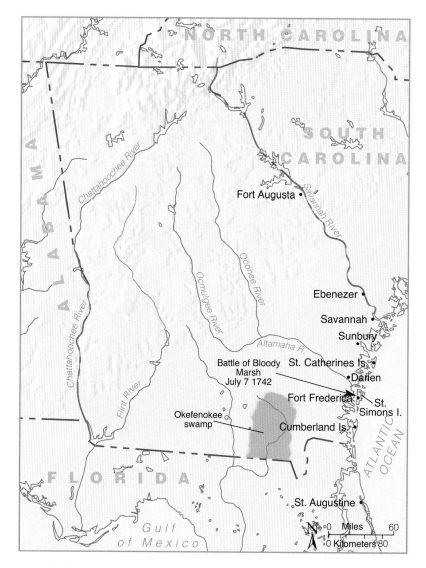

A growing colony.

Oglethorpe led one more attack against St. Augustine the next year, but it, too, failed. Then he had to return to Britain to answer charges that he had performed poorly. Although Parliament cleared him of all charges, he never returned to Georgia. The war dragged on until late 1748. When the European powers made peace, they failed to define the boundary between Georgia and Florida.

During the war years, the colony's population shrank because many people fled for fear of the Spanish. Sephardic Jews who had faced Spanish persecution in Europe were among those who fled. Still, because of Oglethorpe's leadership, the colony survived the first and greatest threat it ever faced from the Spanish in Florida.

6.
EVERYDAY LIFE

The Georgia settlers had three major complaints: rules about landownership; prohibition of hard liquor; and prohibition of slavery. The Trustees had made the rules about land ownership for reasons that made sense in London. The rules made less sense in Georgia. Settlers arriving "on the charity" received fifty acres according to a plan drawn on a map. The Trustees' goal was to create communities that could defend themselves against attack. Too often it turned out that the land was unsuited for farming.

The Savannah River. Streams and rivers served as Georgia's highways. Early settlements were located on navigable streams so that trade goods could be moved easily by boat.

The Trustees also forbade farmers from selling their land. The Trustees' idea was to prevent people from selling their land and squandering all the money, and to prevent wealthy people from buying up land and acquiring huge plantations. This rule particularly annoyed the settlers because it prevented them from acquiring more than 50 acres of land, and from fully owning the land they worked.

For the colony's first eight years the Trustees clung to their landownership rules. But so many settlers complained about the rules and restrictions that controlled where they could live and what they could do with their land that the rules slowly changed. Finally, by 1750, land could be bought, sold, and inherited just like any other commodity. Likewise, the restrictions on hard liquor changed after loud complaints from the settlers. By 1742 the trustees removed the ban on alcohol.

In January 1735, the Trustees decided to prohibit slavery in Georgia because they believed in "the moral value of people doing their own work." They also thought that this would encourage settlement by British Christians. British Christians, in turn, would provide valuable soldiers to guard against the Spanish in Florida. The Georgia settlers looked at the ban on slavery differently. They looked across the border and saw a prosperous South Carolina where owning slaves was the quickest path to wealth. They wanted the same chance to become rich by creating plantations worked by slaves.

THE END OF A VISION

Throughout the Trustee period, Georgia needed laborers. The Trustees had hoped that indentured servants would partially fill this need and then remain in Georgia as

The lighthouse at the entrance to the Savannah River was one of Oglethorpe's first and most useful projects. Built of the best pine, it stood 90 feet (27 meters) tall, a beacon for ships to help them avoid obstacles.

A wealthy planter stands over a newly planted field. A pamphlet for settlers instructed them on how to start a plantation: "If one wants to establish a plantation on previously uncultivated land, one orders the Negroes to clear a piece of land of trees and bushes. ..."

productive citizens. Sometimes this happened but usually it did not. Numerous indentured servants ran off before completing their contracts. A typical master complained that his indentured servants were always sick, in trouble, robbing him, or running off.

In 1750 the Trustees bowed to popular pressure. They decided that Georgians could own slaves and claimed that this decision was made as "an encouragement to the inhabitants." A flood of slave-owning immigrants came to Georgia. Most of them moved into the colony from nearby South Carolina. Just two years after the Trustees conceded the right to own slaves, about 1,000 black slaves were in Georgia along with some 4,000 white people.

A slave cabin. A Georgian cited the "extraordinary heats" as one argument against the ban on slavery, stating that it was, "impossible for white men alone to carry on planting."

Slavery in Georgia

By law, slaves could be forced to work sixteen hours a day. Sunday was supposed to be a rest day, but many masters worked their slaves on Sunday anyway. Slaves of all ages worked: men cut trees, to clear land; while women and children collected and burned brush and tended to crops.

Often slaves received just enough food and clothing to stay alive. A minister described slave life in Georgia: "The upkeep of the [slaves] is cut very sparse. Year in and year out they receive nothing but … corn. Very few receive salt for it, so they cook it in water without salt and lard. If they have benevolent masters … they may receive a little meat a few times a year … in summer [the men] go naked [except for] a cloth rag which hangs from a strap … The women have petticoats; the upper body is bare." Children went without clothes in the summer and all ages went barefoot in the summer.

Georgia had a harsh set of laws, called the slave code. Slaves did not have the same legal rights as whites. They could not travel without written permission, gather in groups off the plantation, or buy or sell goods without special permission. They could be legally executed for destroying crops or helping another slave escape to freedom.

The only thing that protected slaves was the fact that they had economic value just like other tools. Generally, owners did not destroy their tools. In 1770 Georgia's slave population numbered about 10,625.

Shaking rice kernels from the stalks was just one of many jobs that slaves did on Georgia plantations.

Slaves cultivating sugarcane in the West Indies. Many travelers in the southern colonies regarded Georgia slave owners as the most cruel. In part, this was because many Georgia owners originally came from the West Indies where slave treatment was especially severe.

In 1752 the Trustees gave their authority back to the Crown. Georgia became a royal colony.

The Trustee's idealistic vision was gone. Instead of a place where London's poor became **yeoman** farmers and lived in compact, planned villages, Georgia quickly became like South Carolina. A small number of wealthy planters owned huge rice plantations in the **tidewater** where slaves did the work. Most whites worked on struggling farms scattered elsewhere in the colony. Also like the other southern colonies, the tidewater **planters** controlled the political and legal systems.

Until Georgia became a crown colony, it did not have an elected assembly with power to make laws. After the

YEOMAN: FREE MAN WHO OWNS AND WORKS ON A SMALL FARM

TIDEWATER: ANOTHER NAME FOR THE COASTAL LOWLANDS

PLANTER: OWNER OF A LARGE ESTATE, USUALLY FARMED BY SLAVES, CALLED A PLANTATION

A frontier town sketched by a visitor to Georgia. During most of the colonial period, Georgia was very poor. For example, in 1757, historians estimate that fewer than ten people could say that they had 500 pounds [British money] to their name.

British government fully took charge in 1754, Georgia became politically organized like the other colonies. From 1754 until the Revolutionary War it had a royal governor, an appointed council, and a provincial assembly elected by male landowners.

GROWTH OF THE ROYAL COLONY

In 1752 a group of Congregationalists (Puritans) living in South Carolina decided to move to Georgia to make a fresh start. Georgia was between the period of rule by the Trustees and rule by the crown. The Congregationalists took advantage by occupying large tracts of good land that the Trustees had reserved for the "worthy poor." After Georgia became a royal colony, the Congregationalists prospered. By 1771 about

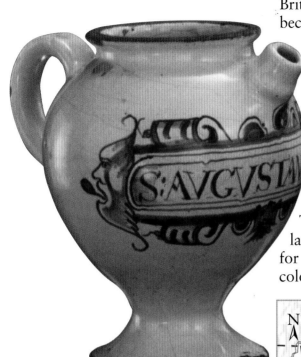

Above: Europeans were unaccustomed to Georgia's hot climate. Its coastal lowlands bred disease-carrying mosquitos and were said to be, "in the spring a paradise, in the summer a hell, and in the autumn a hospital." Apothecaries, or druggists, who sold medicines stored them in jars. Most colonial medicines did not work.

Right: Settlements spread along the coast from Savannah to Darien and up the Savannah River to Augusta. Most people lived in and around Savannah, the Midway-Sunbury region, Darien, Ebenezer, and Augusta.

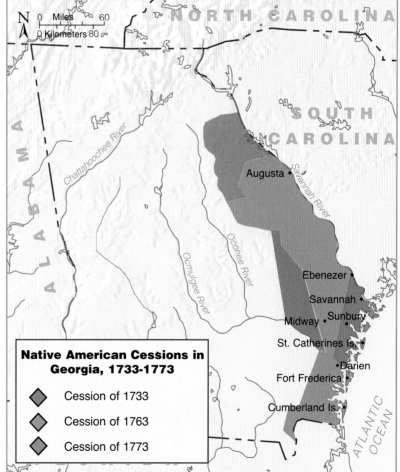

350 Congregationalists lived in Georgia. They owned about 1,500 slaves and possessed about one-third of the wealth of the entire colony.

Sir James Wright served as Lieutenant Governor from 1760 to 1762 and then as Governor until the Revolution drove him from power in 1776. Wright worked with the Georgia assembly to attract new settlers. The assembly offered free land to certain white, European, Christian groups. The lure of free land brought immigrants from Ireland and Quakers from North Carolina. In addition, a steady trickle of individuals continued to move to Georgia. Most were from South Carolina, but some came from the other northern colonies, Bermuda, and Great Britain. For groups and individuals alike, it was the opportunity to acquire large amounts of land that caused them to move to Georgia.

Georgia's colonial leaders believed that the colony's future depended on settling what they called the backcountry, the sparsely populated lands to the west. Governor Wright set to work to persuade the Native Americans to give, or cede, large amounts of land to the white people. He was enormously successful. When he became governor in 1760, Georgia had legal right to

The French and Indian War, 1755 to 1763, had little direct effect on Georgia. This fort guarding the Savannah River never saw action. By the time the war ended, the Spanish had left Florida and the French had left Alabama, so no serious threats remained to the peace of Georgia.

about 1.5 million acres. After Wright completed his negotiations, Georgia had acquired another 5.5 million acres from the Native Americans. The new lands brought new settlers. During Wright's time in office Georgia's population tripled.

Georgia began an economic boom in 1760 that lasted until the Revolutionary War. During this period Georgia had better land to grant to settlers than any other colony. Except for land acquired from the Native Americans in 1773, the land was free. The head of the family received 100 acres with an extra 50 acres for each family member, indentured servant, or slave.

Most Georgia land continued to be used for agriculture. On the frontier were small subsistence farms. People were poor but the land was good, and they could hope to better themselves through hard work. Between the frontier and the coast were family farms and small plantations. These places produced corn, grain, and livestock, particularly cattle. The families provided most of the labor with some assistance from slaves.

Very different were the coastal plantations that grew rice or indigo. Here Georgians made plantations on the South Carolina model using slave labor. Rice became Georgia's most important product. During the royal period, rice made up about one-third of the value of Georgia's exports. The rice trade led to the expansion of port facilities in Savannah and later Sunbury. Indigo and lumber also produced substantial incomes.

The best plantations were located along the tidewater and freshwater swamps that ran inland for about 20 miles (32 kilometers) along rivers and streams.

7.
REVOLUTION

A naturalist, John Bartram, traveled through Georgia in 1765. He wrote in his diary that Governor Wright was "universally respected by all inhabitants. They can hardly say enough in his praise." This attitude changed dramatically when news reached Georgia that Parliament had passed the Stamp Act. Under the Stamp Act, colonists had to pay to have most documents stamped, or risk arrest. Even newspapers had to have stamps. The Stamp Act affected colonists of all social classes. Resistance grew throughout the colonies. In many places riots broke out, and groups calling themselves the Sons of Liberty attacked the offices and homes of tax collectors.

On December 5, 1765, the first stamps arrived in Savannah. Any ship leaving the port needed to purchase a stamp. Governor Wright knew that this was unpopular, so he ordered armed guards to protect the stamps. At the beginning of January, the captain of the guards reported that a mob of "liberty men" had gathered. Wright grabbed a musket and joined his guards to confront the mob. Wright told them that he would

Above: Governor James Wright confronted a mob protesting the Stamp Act and courageously said that their behavior was not "the manner to wait upon the governor." Wright pledged to do his duty to the king by enforcing the Stamp Act. He later issued a decree that forbade patriots to meet and discuss their "imaginary grievances," but they defied him and met anyway.

Right: A view of colonial Savannah after several decades of growth. In 1761, Savannah loaded 42 ships for sea trade. Because of the expansion of the rice trade, in 1765 the port loaded 153 ships.

enforce the Stamp Act. Several days of tension followed. Soldiers guarded the stamps and Wright set up a force of merchants, clerks, and sailors to patrol the streets. Meanwhile, the liberty men met at taverns and talked about what to do.

Wright's firm leadership enabled merchants and the protestors to reach an understanding. The ships stuck in port purchased stamps so they could leave. This marked the only time that any of the thirteen colonies purchased stamps. As news of the Stamp Act spread, liberty men living in the backcountry gathered for a march on Savannah. They arrived on February 4, 1766, carrying guns and beating drums. But again Wright gathered an armed force to oppose them. The liberty men backed down before any violence occurred.

Unlike other royal governors, Wright succeeded because he wisely planned ahead. He worked with important local leaders and avoided making proclamations and threats that would anger people. Still, from the time of the Stamp Act until the outbreak of the Revolutionary War, conflict focused on the question of who had the right to impose taxes on the colonies.

A number of events took place over the next ten years to inflame **patriots** in the thirteen colonies. They included various tax measures such as the tea tax that led to the Boston Tea Party in December 1773. Great Britain responded to the Boston Tea Party by closing the port of Boston and placing Massachusetts under military rule. The British goal was to teach all the colonies to submit to British rule. Patriots throughout the American colonies called the various British laws the Coercive Acts, or the Intolerable Acts.

Increasing numbers of people argued that they would have to fight for independence from Great Britain. However, during these years Georgia was prospering. In addition, Governor Wright was continuing to acquire land from the Native Americans so the colony could expand westward. Most Georgians were reluctant to risk this prosperity. Georgia did not send any delegates to the First Continental Congress held in Philadelphia in September 1774.

In January 1775, five of Georgia's twelve **parishes** voted to send delegates to the Second Continental Congress. Because a majority did not agree, no Georgia delegates

> PARISH: LOCAL GOVERNMENT DISTRICT BASED ON A CHURCH DISTRICT
>
> PATRIOT: AMERICAN WHO WANTED THE COLONIES TO BE INDEPENDENT OF GREAT BRITAIN

Georgian patriots sent Dr. Lyman Hall to the Second Continental Congress in Philadelphia with 200 barrels of rice and 50 British pounds in cash for the relief of the Boston poor. Later Hall was one of three Georgians who signed the Declaration of Independence.

Georgia was deeply divided over loyalty to King George III.

initially attended this second congress. In addition, while the other colonies agreed to boycott trade with Great Britain, most of Georgia remained open to such trade.

News of the battle of Lexington and Concord, Masachusetts, which took place on April 19, 1775, reached Savannah on May 10, 1775. That next night a mob stole most of the gunpowder stored at the public powder magazine. On June 2 they damaged the cannons in Savannah in order to prevent them from being used to salute the king's birthday. Yet on June 5 Governor Wright, his council, and other gentlemen drank to the king's health under the flagpole. Nearby, patriots built a liberty pole and then went to a tavern to have their own celebration. Georgia was divided but still peaceful.

The patriots slowly gained control of Georgia. They smuggled in gunpowder, freed a smuggling ship that the governor had seized, and took weapons from public storehouses. In Charles Town, South Carolina, patriots intercepted and opened Governor Wright's mail. They took his letters that described his troubles and replaced them with letters saying everything was fine. In this way they worked to prevent any British soldiers from being sent to help the royal governor. By July, Wright concluded that the colony was lost to the rebels. Georgia patriots

LOYALIST: COLONIST WHO WANTED AMERICA TO REMAIN A COLONY OF GREAT BRITAIN

GUERRILLA: SPANISH FOR "LITTLE WAR"; REFERS TO A TYPE OF WARFARE INVOLVING SURPRISE ATTACKS BY SMALL GROUPS OF FIGHTERS. GUERRILLA FIGHTERS ARE CALLED GUERRILLAS.

French and American troops tried and failed to recapture Savannah from these siege lines in 1779.

ended the old royal colonial government and took control during the summer of 1775. They elected delegates to the Second Continental Congress and told them to work to preserve American rights and liberties. With these actions, Georgia formally joined the rebelling colonies.

During the Revolutionary War, the border between Georgia and Florida became a British and **loyalist** stronghold. Georgia patriot troops raided the area and made three unsuccessful attempts to capture British-held St. Augustine. The British invaded Georgia and captured Savannah in December 1778. A French naval fleet carrying French soldiers arrived off Savannah in September 1779 and American troops marched from South Carolina to join them, but the combined force was unable to recapture the town. For the rest of the war the British controlled the coast and the rebels dominated the backcountry. Rebels and loyalists fought one another in a savage **guerrilla** war in the backcountry. Although the British lost the last major battle of the Revolution at Yorktown, Virginia, in October 1781, British troops did not evacuate Savannah until it became clear that a peace treaty would be signed. The British army left Georgia in July 1782, taking along several thousand loyalists and former slaves who had helped the British side.

EPILOGUE

Georgia became the fourth state to approve the United States Constitution on January 2, 1788. Savannah remained the state capital until 1785, when the capital was moved to Augusta, Georgia's second oldest city. Augusta remained the capital for ten years. Atlanta is the state's capital and largest city today. Georgia's other large cities include Columbus, Savannah, and Macon.

Much of Georgia's land was cleared of trees to create fields for farms and plantations. Cotton became Georgia's most important crop before the Civil War. Trees have since been permitted to return to much of the land. Lumber, paper products, and turpentine, made from the sap of pine trees, have replaced cotton in importance as products of Georgia.

Of the state's 8 million people, about 71% are white, 27% African Americans, and the remaining 2% are Native American, Hispanic, or Asian. As in South Carolina, a group of blacks of West African descent lived on Georgia's sea islands, isolated from the rest of the state. They developed their own culture and a language called Gullah, a mix of colonial English and several West African languages.

Fewer than 3% of Georgia's people work in agriculture, and more than 20% work in manufacturing. Georgia is the nation's largest producer of peanuts. Other farm products include poultry, eggs, cattle, milk, tobacco, cotton, corn, and peaches. Georgia is famous for its peaches. Major manufactured products include textiles,

In the decades before the Civil War, cotton, grown and tended by slaves, became an important crop in Georgia.

carpet, food products, electronic equipment, airplanes, and cars and trucks.

The state's pre-Revolutionary history is on display at several sites. As Georgia's first and oldest existing town, Savannah is still laid out as it was in Oglethorpe's day, and many of the original squares survive, along with a few colonial buildings. On St. Simons Island, the Bloody Marsh Memorial Site commemorates Oglethorpe's battle with the Spanish. Also on the island is Fort Frederica National Monument, which has the ruins of the early colonial fort. A reconstruction of Fort King George is offered at a state historic site near Darien. Ancient Native American mounds, deserted long before the first Europeans arrived, still exist at the Ocmulgee National Monument.

Atlanta, in northeastern Georgia, is the state capitol. It is a thriving cultural and business center. The striking architectural forms pictured are of the Peachtree Center in downtown Atlanta.

DATELINE

1540: Spanish explorer Hernando de Soto leads a military expedition through Georgia.

1565: The Spanish settle St. Augustine, Florida, and claim land that includes Georgia.

1566: The Spanish build a fort and Spanish priests found missions on islands off the coast of Georgia.

1702: South Carolina colonists begin conducting raids on Native American allies of the Spanish in Georgia.

1721: South Carolinians build a fort in Georgia, but abandon it four years later.

1732: A group of 21 Trustees receive a charter and a land grant to found a colony in Georgia.

NOVEMBER 17, 1732 – FEBRUARY 12, 1733: The first colonists sail from England to Georgia under the leadership of James Oglethorpe.

1734: Religious refugees from Salzburg, Austria, arrive in Georgia.

1735: Moravians arrive to settle in Georgia. By 1740 most move to Pennsylvania.

1740: British and colonial troops led by Oglethorpe begin an unsuccessful siege of St. Augustine in Spanish Florida.

1742: Oglethorpe and his troops repulse a Spanish invasion of Georgia.

1743: Oglethorpe leads another failed siege against St. Augustine. He is recalled to Britain to account for his failures, although he is cleared of charges..

1750: The Trustees end their ban on slavery in Georgia.

1752: The Trustees give up control of Georgia, and Georgia becomes a royal colony.

1775: Georgia patriots abolish the royal government of Georgia and set up their own government. The following year, the new government formally declares its independence from Great Britain.

DECEMBER 1778: British troops capture Savannah.

SEPTEMBER 1779: American and French troops lay siege to Savannah but fail to recapture it.

JULY 1782: The last British troops leave Georgia.

JANUARY 2, 1788: Georgia becomes the fourth state to approve the United States Constitution.

GLOSSARY

AMERICA: land that contains the continents of North America and South America

ARCHBISHOP: high-ranking minister who has authority over a church district

ASSEMBLY: lower house of a legislature, with delegates elected by the voters

CAMPAIGN: series of actions taken to reach a military goal

CHARTER: document containing the rules for running an organization

CONGREGATIONAL: church organized by Puritans, based on the idea that each congregation governed itself without interference from a central authority

COUNCIL: group of advisors, similar to the upper house of a legislature, appointed by a colonial governor

DEBTOR: person who owes a debt, usually money

GARRISON: soldiers stationed at a fort to protect it

GREAT BRITAIN: nation formed by England, Wales, Scotland, and Northern Ireland; "Great Britain" came into use when England and Scotland formally unified in 1707.

GUERRILLA: Spanish for "little war"; refers to a type of warfare involving surprise attacks by small groups of fighters. Guerrilla fighters are called guerrillas.

INDENTURED SERVANT: person who has agreed to work as a servant for a certain number of years in exchange for food, clothing, a place to sleep, and payment of one's passage across the Atlantic to the colonies

INDIANS: name given to all Native Americans at the time Europeans first came to America, because it was believed that America was actually a close neighbor of India

INQUISITION: state-sponsored persecution of non-Catholics in Spain and Portugal, noted for the use of torture

LOYALIST: colonist who wanted America to remain a colony of Great Britain

LUTHERAN: belonging to the Protestant church based on the ideas of Martin Luther, a 16th-century German monk who questioned Catholicism

MILITIA: group of citizens, not normally part of the army, who join together to defend their land in an emergency

MISSION: place in a foreign land established by people trying to spread their religion, usually Christianity

MORAVIAN: member of a Christian church first formed in Moravia, in eastern Europe, during the 1400s

NEW WORLD: western hemisphere of the earth, including North America, Central America, and South America; so called because the people of the Old World, in the east, did not know about the existence of the Americas until the 1400s. The Old World consists of Europe, Asia, and Africa.

PACIFIST: person against war and violence; the beliefs of such a person

PARISH: local government district based on a church district

PARLIAMENT: legislature of Great Britain; it has an upper house, the House of Lords, and a lower house, the House of Commons

PATRIOT: American who wanted the colonies to be independent of Great Britain

PLANTER: owner of a large estate, usually farmed by slaves, called a plantation

PROTESTANT: member of any Christian church that has broken from away from Roman Catholic or Eastern Orthodox control

SIEGE: campaign to capture a place by surrounding it, cutting it off from supplies, and attacking it

TIDEWATER: another name for the coastal lowlands

TRUSTEES: group of people entrusted with the management of an organization or a piece of property

UTOPIA: imaginary place with a perfect society and government

WEST INDIES: islands of the Caribbean Sea, so called because the first European visitors thought they were near India

YEOMAN: free man who owns and works on a small farm

FURTHER READING

Branch, Muriel Miller. *The Water Brought Us: The Story of the Gullah-speaking People*. New York: Cobblehill Books, 1995.

Davis, Harold E. *The Fledgling Province: Social and Cultural Life in Colonial Georgia, 1733–1776*. Chapel Hill: University of North Carolina Press, 1976.

Lommel, Cookie, and Arthur Meier Schlesinger. *James Oglethorpe: Humanitarian and Soldier*. Philadelphia: Chelsea House, 2000.

Long, Cathryn J. *The Cherokee*. San Diego: Lucent Books, 2000.

Smith, Carter, ed. *Battles in a New Land: A Source Book on Colonial America*. Brookfield, Conn.: Millbrook Press, 1991.

Smith, Carter, ed. *Daily Life: A Source Book on Colonial America*. Brookfield, Conn.: Millbrook Press, 1991.

Smith, Carter, ed. *Explorers and Settlers: A Source Book on Colonial America*. Brookfield, Conn.: Millbrook Press, 1991.

Websites

http://www.americaslibrary.gov
Select "Jump back in time" for links to history activities

http://www.georgia.gov
This site has links to Georgia history sites

Disclaimer
All Internet addresses (URLs) given in this book were valid at the time it went to press. However, due to the dynamic nature of the Internet, some addresses may have changed, or sites may have ceased to exist since publication. While the author and publisher regret any inconvenience this may cause readers, no responsibility for any such changes can be accepted by either the author or the publisher.

Bibliography

Coleman, Kenneth. *Colonial Georgia: A History*. New York: Charles Scribner's Sons, 1976.

Gallay, Alan. *Voices of the Old South: Eyewitness Accounts, 1528–1861*. Athens: University of Georgia Press, 1994.

Middleton, Richard. *Colonial America: A History, 1607–1760*. Cambridge, Mass: Blackwell, 1992.

Taylor, Alan. *American Colonies*. New York: Viking, 2001.

The American Heritage History of the Thirteen Colonies. New York: American Heritage Publishing Co., 1967.

INDEX